CONTENTS

Published in Great Britain by Stafford Pemberton Publishing
Co. Ltd., The Ruskin Chambers, Drury Lane, Knutsford,
Cheshire WA16 6HA
Printed and bound in Italy
ISBN 0 86030 186 9

Stafford Pemberton Publishing

Action Man

annual 1980

New Irel
Kapsu
Lavongai
Byron Str
Sandwich I
Namatanai
Rabaul
5°
Bismarck
Arch.
St George
Ch
Kikopo
NEA
C. Orford
Jacquinot B.
C. Hollmann
Stettin B.

INFERNO!

By the end of June, 1943, the great Japanese base at Rabaul, on the island of New Britain, 5° south of the equator and just to the east of Papua and New Guinea, was one of the main causes of concern for the allies.

Although the allies were making progress by invading some of the smaller islands in the area and taking over airstrips from which they could launch their attacks on Rabaul, it was decided by the British High Command that something must be done to greatly reduce the effectiveness of the base.

In the first week of July, Action Man and G.I. Joe were dropped by parachute over New Georgia Island. They met up with Major Jeff Anders, who was to brief them, and give them any assistance Action Man thought necessary.

"Good to see you, Action Man," said the tough looking little Major, "we sure could use a couple more like you round here."

Action Man looked at the bags under the Major's eyes and the thick, dirty stubble on his chin.

"You look like you've been keeping pretty busy," he said.

"You ain't kiddin'. We've been island hoppin' and jumpin' in and out of boats for weeks. We're doin' all right but we got to do something about the Japanese base at Rabaul before we can go any farther . . . That's why you and your partner are here . . ."

Action Man warmed to the Major's enthusiasm.

"You've got a plan?" He asked. The Major nodded.

"Well let's have a look and see what we can make of it." Action Man was always eager to help the allied advance. The Major moved away from the drawings on the operations desk. He scratched the bridge of his nose and gestured toward the docks.

"You'll be moving out tomorrow night. You'll be in a normal sub, with a midget sub in tow. There's word of a big sea battle brewing off here and the strategists figure it's really gonna erupt tomorrow night. That means you've got a chance of slipping in while everyone else is trying to blow each other up."

The Major was right. Early next night, while the sea battle raged offshore, Action Man and G.I. Joe boarded the sub that was to take them close to Rabaul.

G.I. Joe checked out his new quarters.

"Where do they keep the midget sub then?" He asked.

Action man smiled. G.I. Joe had the most up to date weaponry the American Army could supply, but he still didn't understand something until he saw how it worked.

"So that's what you've been looking for is it?" laughed Action Man. "You won't find it inside the sub – it's being towed behind."

"Seems like a bit of a waste to me, sending this big thing out as well – why didn't we just set off from New Georgia in the midget then these guys could have stayed to fight in the big sea battle?"

Action Man's smile disappeared, but his easy manner remained.

"The trouble is, Joe, that these midgets are much slower than ordinary subs. They can only make two or three knots and their range is pretty limited to say the least. We'll have to be dead on target or we won't be able to get back out again at all."

G.I. Joe threw his cigar to the floor and laughed bitterly.

"Now you tell me," he said, "it's spooky enough down here in this big one without having to worry about a cramped little ship that's liable to run out of fuel."

Joe's speech was cut short by the opening of a hatch and the appearance of Submarine Captain Roger McGuinn, a lean, hard man, with thick spectacles and an off hand, irritable manner. Captain McGuinn smiled.

"We're going up to see if it's clear for you to transfer to the Midget. Do you boys want to take a look?"

Action Man put down the gun he had been cleaning.

"Thanks Captain – I have always wanted to look through a periscope."

"And I always wanted to shout 'UP PERISCOPE!" interrupted G.I. Joe. "How about it, Captain?"

Captain McGuinn nodded and G.I. Joe bellowed his order. The periscope went up and Action Man did a full sweep to make sure there was no enemy shipping around. Seeing that they were alone, Action Man turned and studied the shoreline, some two miles away.

"How does it look?" asked McGuinn.

"The coast is clear." replied Action Man.

"Then let's get going!" laughed G.I. Joe.

Action Man and G.I. Joe changed into their frogmen's outfits and set off for the midget sub. The special equipment they would need for the raid was already packed in waterproof bags inside the tiny submarine.

The water was cold, but neither Action Man or G.I. Joe felt it. Joe released the towing line and Action Man swam over the tiny hatch and set about opening it. It sprang open as Joe swam over, and they squeezed into the narrow airlock before taking their places in the cramped interior.

Action Man took the controls while Joe sat behind. Soon the small but powerful engines were taking them towards Rabaul. As they neared the coast they entered an area of mines, secured to the sea bottom by chains. The mines bristled with plungers and Action Man knew that sufficient pressure on any one of the plungers would mean the end of the mission. The greater manoeuvrability of the midget sub enabled him to weave his way safely through the deadly planted bombs. Dawn was breaking when he steered the sub into a narrow inlet. Rabaul was within striking distance, and Action Man and G.I. Joe intended to strike.

After steering the sub into the shadow of some tall, sharp rocks, Action Man prepared to go ashore. Joe passed him his special waterproof bag and he peeled off his frogman's suit and unzipped the bag, looking for something more suitable for Jungle warfare. Action Man and Joe dressed swiftly, not bothering to speak as they put on their denims, checked their stens, hung grenades from their web belts and laced up their special rope soled boots that enabled them to tread more quietly through the deadly jungle.

But their bags were far from empty, and they slung them over their backs, waded to the shore and set off through the damp undergrowth, leaving the sand and sea and going to meet the war inland. They travelled in silence, with both men fully alert and continually looking around and above for any sign of danger, anything that might re-affirm the fact they knew only too well – they were not alone. Every so often Action Man would hold out his arm as a signal to stop and they would both stand stock still, eyes darting and ears pricked for any tell-tale noises. It was while they were standing in such a position that they saw their first Japanese soldiers.

Action Man said nothing. He drew his

Commando knife as he heard Japanese voices approaching along the trail and G.I. Joe silently did likewise. The voices came closer.

Action Man signalled G.I. Joe not to make any move. He was sure that the Japanese did not know of their presence. The voices, subdued and angry, passed closely by and Action Man crawled stealthily forward to see the Japanese soldiers disappearing along the trail. He lay watching as Joe made his way silently to his side.

"Seems like they're not used to visitors," said Joe, his knife still at the ready. "They'd be much quieter than that in a combat zone. We could take them easy."

"Maybe," answered Action Man. "But if we start leaving dead bodies around here, we aren't going to make it to Rabaul."

Joe checked his ammunition with an air of impatience.

"You're right," he said, "but I'll save a few rounds in case we meet them on the way back."

They headed onward through the tough country. Action Man had seen a hill on the map that should give them a good vantage point for the Japanese base. They could spy out the land and then move in soon after nightfall. He was about to tell Joe when they came to a sudden clearing and found themselves face to face with three Japanese soldiers.

The Japanese didn't have time to look surprised, never mind raise their guns, before Action Man and G.I. Joe were upon them. Action Man's knife plunged into the Japanese Corporal's chest as G.I. Joe's gun butt flattened his comrade. The third man was laid flat by a deadly kick to the throat from Action Man's rope soled jungle boot.

As they dragged the three lifeless bodies into the thick undergrowth, G.I. Joe spoke with the bitter pride of a professional having done his job well.

"We hit them fast and we hit them hard – just like the training book says." He said, releasing the limp arms of the unconscious Japanese soldier.

"Yeah, Joe, we did," said Action Man, dropping the body he was dragging. "But most important, we kept it quiet." He arranged the leaves so the bodies could not be seen from the trail. "Now let's get up that hill and see what we've got to do."

The hill was a tough climb and they had to use their machettes to clear a way through the undergrowth. At least the new trail they forged meant they were unlikely to meet any Japanese.

By mid-afternoon they were at the top of the hill. Action Man left the undergrowth to find a suitable reconnaissance position. He returned to lead Joe to a small rocky outcrop with an ideal view of Rabaul, which was right on the North East tip of the island. Action Man took the binoculars from his pack and carefully and methodically surveyed the base. G.I. Joe took advantage of the break to prepare some food and then rest his tired muscles after the long trek.

"The fuel dump's the thing to hit," said Action Man as he swallowed the last of the beans Joe had cooked. "We blow a couple of those tanks and the fire will set the rest of them off. It'll be a chain reaction, everything that can burn will be alight. In the confusion we can nobble the communications building."

G.I. Joe checked the grenades he was carrying.

"Let's get in there," he smiled, "wanna check the stuff?"

Action Man nodded and the two men emptied their bags. They went quickly through their armaments.

"Plastic explosives, time fuses, heavy tape, wire cutters . . ." Action Man flipped

his bag closed, and reloaded his sten. "I think we've got enough."

The sun had just set and as in all tropical countries, when the sun goes down, it gets dark very quickly. The two men set off slowly down the hill, making use of whatever cover they could find. The Japanese had cleared the slopes of vegetation and although that made the going much easier than on the way up the hill, they had to crawl long distances to avoid being seen by the Japanese guards. Eventually they came to the perimeter fence.

The two brave men dropped down flat on their stomachs and moved forwards using their elbows and pushing with the inside of their knees in an expert demonstration of the 'leopard crawl' that was so vital to jungle fighters.

There were four barbed wire fences and they could see three guards patrolling inside. The guards were obviously not expecting any trouble as Action Man and G.I. Joe clearly heard two of them laughing and exchanging insults at the far end of the large open space which seemed to serve as a parade ground. The third guard made his way slowly up past their hiding place at the corner of the compound and then turned to make his way lazily back to his two comrades. As he did so, Action Man slid forward, quickly cutting the bottom wire of all four fences. With G.I. Joe at his side, they edged slowly into the shadow of a small hut. There were voices coming from inside the hut but Action Man's forefinger, pressed close to his lips, told Joe that there was to be no attack on the building . . . yet.

Using what little cover was offered, and taking full advantage of the Japanese Soldiers' complacency, Action Man and G.I. Joe advanced on the fuel tanks, Action Man going first while Joe covered him, and then Action Man lifted the sten to cover Joe as he ran to safety.

The fuel dump was bathed in bright light from six floodlights and watchtowers at each corner of the compound meant that any intruder had to be very careful indeed. Action Man watched the guard in the nearest tower until he turned away, then he nudged Joe and they sprinted at a low crouch into the dark shadow cast by the first of the huge fuel tanks.

Action Man signalled Joe to start taping explosives to this tank while he moved on to another further inside the dump. Within minutes they were both speedily taping large packages of explosives onto the metal tanks. Action Man set his fuse for three minutes, then rejoined Joe as he set his fuse for two minutes.

"All set?" Whispered Action Man. Joe finished setting his fuse, picked up his gun and nodded. The time for caution had passed. Now their main job was to get out alive. With their fingers on the triggers of their stens they started running.

They dashed between two wooden buildings, hoping that they would not meet any Japanese soldiers. They were out of luck. Six Japanese soldiers stood at the end of the alley.

At the sound of running feet the Japanese soldiers turned, but even as they lifted their guns to fire, Action Man and G.I. Joe travelling at top speed, cut them down with a sustained burst from their stens. They leapt over the Japanese bodies even as they were falling and headed straight on.

The gunfire had raised the alarm and Japanese soldiers were pouring out of all the buildings. The Tannoy started up and Action Man and G.I. Joe found themselves running into a square between the buildings with Japanese soldiers on every side. Without stopping, Action Man and G.I. Joe each took a grenade from their belts and pulled the pins out with their teeth. Action Man threw to the left and Joe hurled his grenade to the right, then they both set

about shooting a way through the Japanese soldiers in front of them.

The grenades exploded almost simultaneously, there was some answering firepower and then the first of the tanks went up. There was a hot, rushing wind and Action Man and G.I. Joe hurled themselves to the floor. The heat burned the back of their heads and burning fuel rained all around them. As they buried their faces deep in the dirt of the compound, the second tank blew. There was a deep dull explosion and then a roaring sound as the burning fuel spilled onto the ground, spreading towards the other buildings and the other tanks.

The Japanese had all but abandoned their search for the two soldiers, and they fought desperately to halt the spread of flames that already licked round the many timber frame buildings in the compound. Action Man looked back to see about fifty Japanese soldiers silhouetted against a huge wall of flame, reaching hundreds of feet into the black night and casting an orange-red glow on the frantic activity on the ground.

They made their way to a building that had a large mast on the roof.

"This is the communications building Joe," said Action Man as Japanese soldiers with headphones on peered out anxiously into the night. As another massive explosion rocked the night and a third fuel tank blew up, the one guard on the doorway left his post and ran to help his comrades fight the blaze. Action Man ran into the building and raced up the stairs three at a time. As he neared the top he pulled the pin from a grenade and kicked open the door with a mighty blow from his heavy boot. The door slammed back on its hinges and Action Man just had time to roll the grenade towards the largest bank of instruments, before it swung back shut again, muffling the explosion within.

Action Man re-opened the door to check that the damage had been done. The room was totally wrecked, and the highly sophisticated communications equipment was a smouldering tangle of useless valves and wires. The one Japanese soldier still alive was wandering round the room, completely dazed and deafened by the effects of the explosion in such a confined space.

"Come on buddy," said a voice at Action Man's shoulder, "I think we've given them enough to think about for one day." Action Man patted Joe lightly on the arm and the two of them ran swiftly and silently down the stairs and started heading for the beach.

They went out as they had come in, wriggling under the cut wire fences, but this time there was less danger, with the majority of Japanese soldiers being involved in the futile battle to stop the fire spreading further. Even so, they were a good half mile from the camp before they stopped to take a look at their handiwork.

"Makes the 4th of July look kinda tame, don't it Action Man," said G.I. Joe, a big smile splitting his dirty, smoke blackened face.

"Looks like another successful night's work," Action Man replied quietly. He hefted his sten from one hand to the other, and turned his back at the raging inferno. "Let's go."

Twelve hours later, they made their rendezvous with the submarine which was to take them back to New Georgia island. Captain McGuinn was there to help them aboard.

"Nice work." He said. "Some of the boys figured this one was too tough even for you, Action Man."

G.I. Joe spat out a stream of sea water.

"Don't bet against Action Man unless you wanna lose your money." He said firmly.

THE FRENCH CONNECTION
A DESERTED BAY IN NORTHERN FRANCE. FOUR DINGHIES SLIP AWAY FROM A DARKENED FISHING BOAT. ABOARD THE CRAFT ARE ACTION MAN, ERNIE PERKINS, SIX RESISTANCE MEN, A MORTAR AND 100 POUNDS OF EXPLOSIVES. THEIR OBJECTIVE – A DRY DOCK SIX MILES ALONG THE COAST. SUDDENLY –
RArrrrrrr- SPKTUFF - RArrr
LOOK!
A PLANE! SOUNDS LIKE IT'S IN TROUBLE.
IT'S A LANC!
AND IT'S COMING DOWN RIGHT IN THE MIDDLE OF OUR ROUTE TO THE DOCK – THE GERMANS WILL BE EVERYWHERE.
ACTION MAN'S JUDGEMENT IS SPOT ON... THE SOUND OF RENDING METAL TELLS THEM THE PLANE HAS COME DOWN...
NO EXPLOSION – THAT MEANS THE CREW MIGHT STILL BE ALIVE WE MUST HELP THEM.
NO! WE MUST NOT FORGET THE MISSION. YOU GO UP THAT WAY. WE WILL GO ROUND HERE TO SEE IF THERE IS ANYONE LEFT TO SAVE –
WE WILL MEET YOU CLOSE TO THE BARN OF THE SECOND FARM ON THE ROAD.
ACTION MAN AND ERNIE TAKE TO THE CLIFFS, HOPING TO BYPASS THE DOWNED LANCASTER. AFTER SEVERAL MINUTES...
UNH...
WHAT'S THAT?
OVER THERE! SOMEONE'S HURT!
IT'S THE LANCASTER PILOT!
JERRIES... HUNDREDS OF THEM. CAPTURED THE CREW. I... UNH... I WAS THROWN CLEAR.
THE RESISTANCE MEN ARE WALKING STRAIGHT INTO A TRAP. WE'VE GOT TO WARN THEM. COME ON!

AS ACTION MAN AND ERNIE RACE TO WARN THEM, THE RESISTANCE FIGHTERS, UNAWARE OF WHAT HAS HAPPENED, COME ACROSS THE STRICKEN LANCASTER...
EVERYTHING'S QUIET. DOESN'T LOOK LIKE THERE'S ANY SURVIVORS.
WAIT!... IN THE COCKPIT— THERE'S SOMEONE MOVING! SOMEONE'S ALIVE IN THERE!
THERE IS SOMEONE VERY MUCH ALIVE IN THE COCKPIT – A GERMAN!
COME CLOSER FRENCHMEN... LET MY SOLDIERS GET A GOOD SHOT AT YOU.
BUT, BEFORE THE GERMANS CAN OPEN FIRE...
GET BACK! IT'S A TRAP! THE PLACE IS CRAWLING WITH GERMANS.
RATTATTATTAT!
IT'S ACTION MAN GET BACK!
BOOM!
BLANG!
ATTATTATTA!
AAARGH!
THE RESISTANCE MEN REGAIN THEIR COVER AS FIERCE FIGHTING ERUPTS...
ACTION MAN AND ERNIE FIGHT THEIR WAY TO THE RESISTANCE FIGHTERS' POSITION...
IT'S NO USE! THERE'S TOO MANY OF THEM. WE'LL NEVER GET TO THE DOCK.
MAYBE NOT, BUT WE'RE NOT FINISHED YET. MAKE YOUR WAY BACK TO THE BEACH. WE'LL MEET YOU ON THE SHORE. THE LANC'S PILOT WILL BE THERE.
AS THE RESISTANCE MEN PULL BACK, ACTION MAN AND ERNIE POUR OUT A STREAM OF RED HOT LEAD...
AIM FOR THE LANC'S FUEL TANKS AND BE READY TO RUN!
BLANG-AG-AG-AG!

ACTION MAN'S AIM IS TRUE ...
KA-BROOOM!
LET'S GO!
STILL PURSUED BY GERMAN FORCES ACTION MAN AND ERNIE REACH THE SHORE...
NOT IF WE CAN SIGNAL THE MEN ON BOARD FIRST
STREWTH! MORE GERMANS! THEY'RE BOUND TO GET THE BOAT.
ACTION MAN SIGNALS A BRIEF MORSE MESSAGE AND THE TWO FREEDOM FIGHTERS STILL ON THE FISHING BOAT SLIP OVER THE SIDE...
AS THE BRAVE BAND OF FIGHTERS REGROUP ON THE SHORE...
THAT COULD BE USEFUL. SET UP THE MORTAR.
THEY'VE SEEN HER. LOOKS LIKE THEY'RE GOING TO BOARD.
LEAVING ONLY A SKELETON CREW ON BOARD THEIR OWN VESSEL, THE GERMANS LAUNCH A BOARDING PARTY...
WE'VE ONLY TIME FOR A COUPLE OF SHOTS— BETTER MAKE THEM COUNT!
WHOOOMPH!
NOW!

ACTION MAN LEADS THE ASSAULT ON THE GERMAN BOAT...
KEEP FIRING! DON'T LET THEM GET THE ENGINE STARTED!
RATATATA!
THE GERMANS HOLD ON VALIANTLY...
FIRE! BLOW THESE LUNATICS OUT OF THE WATER!
DUK-UDUKUDUK!
BUT THE SPEED OF THE ATTACK IS TOO MUCH...
AKRASH!
THE BOAT IS TAKEN...
THE GERMANS! THEY'RE ON THE CLIFF!
IT'S TOO LATE FOR THAT. THIS IS OUR PASSPORT TO THE DRY DOCK... GET HER GOING!
YOU CAN SLOW DOWN, WE'RE OUT OF RANGE
THEY'VE GOT A RADIO. EXPECT A BIG WELCOME!
WITH ACTION MAN AT THE HELM THEY SET OFF FOR THE DRY DOCK...
SURE ENOUGH...
CRIPES! LET'S HOPE THAT GUN STILL WORKS!
SACRE BLEU!

IT DOES...
YOU'VE HIT HIM!
UKKA-DUKKA-DUKKA!
GOOD SHOOTING, ERNIE.
IT'S NOT FINISHED YET – LOOK!
SPPPUPPPALASH!
STRAP THE EXPLOSIVES ON THE FRONT. MAYBE WE CAN OUTRUN THEM AND RAM THE DRY DOCK.
S9
THE GERMANS ARE FAR FROM BEATEN...
FIRE ONE AND TWO!
S16
ACTION MAN IS ALERT TO THE DANGER...
TIN FISH FRONT AND BACK ...JUST ONE CHANCE...
ACTION MAN TURNS QUICKLY...
GOOD STEERING CAPTAIN! THEY'VE GONE EITHER SIDE!
STAY COOL, ERNIE WE'RE GOING TO TAKE THIS SHIP–
GET FIRING!

THEY CUT IN FRONT OF THE GERMAN SHIP...
O.K. MEN GET ABOARD!
AKADAKADAKA!
BLOOOM!
LOOK OUT!
THERE IS SOME FIERCE HAND TO HAND FIGHTING
COME ON! DON'T LET THEM STOP YOU!
THE GERMANS FINALLY SURRENDER...
WE'VE GOT TWO BOATS NOW, WE CAN STRAP THE WHEEL DOWN AND SEND THE OTHER ONE STRAIGHT IN – WITH THE EXPLOSIVES STRAPPED TO THE FRONT.
DEAD RIGHT, ERNIE, BUT FIRST WE SOFTEN THEM UP WITH A FEW TORPEDOES.
FIRE ONE! FIRE TWO! RELEASE CRAFT AND HEAD FOR HOME!
AS THE DRY DOCK IS BREACHED...
SKI-BOOANG!
LOOKS LIKE WE DID IT AFTER ALL, ACTION MAN.
YEAH – NOW WE'VE GOT TO MAKE SURE WE DON'T GET SHOT UP BY OUR OWN SIDE!

The Sten Gun

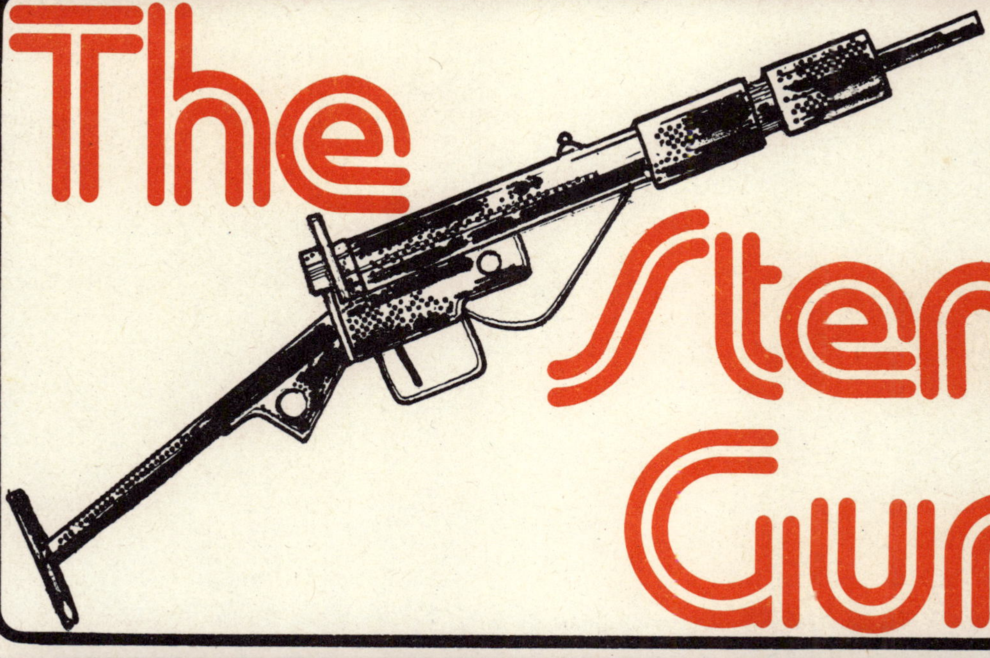

In 1940 the British Army was in desperate need of a standard, reliable sub-machine gun with which it could arm its troops. They had been importing the famous Thompson gun popularised by Al Capone, but this, apart from being in short supply, was both too expensive and too slow to repair. With prolonged fighting on the ground seeming more and more likely, it was imperative that the English soldier should be as effectively armed as his German counterpart, and it was R. Shepherd and H. Turpin who came to the rescue.

The Sten gun was 762mm long, with a barrel of 197mm and a calibre of 9mm. Its 32 round magazine fired 9 rounds every second, and, unloaded, the Sten weighed 2.8 Kg. It was effective up to 200 metres.

The first Stens had their critics who said the gun was crude, cheap and dangerous, citing the lack of an effective safety catch as being its biggest drawback. Indeed the Sten *was* simple and unsophisticated, but it was functional, the parts could be easily manufactured and replaced, and the average soldier wasn't so fussy if he had a gun that worked. Stens went into mass production, and as well as arming British soldiers they were shipped to resistance fighters throughout Europe. They were particularly effective in street fighting.

Various modifications to the original design were made and the Sten Mark 11 came out. More than two million of these guns were produced and by the end of the war Stens were comparable with anything the German Army was using in the Front Line. The much maligned Sten may have started life humbly, but it went out in a blaze of glory, and it wasn't until the 1960s that the British Army stopped using them.

DEATH OF A GIANT

The Battle of the Coral Sea in 1942 was the first battle in Naval history to be fought between two fleets – the Americans and the Japanese – who never came in sight of one another. For the first time, the extreme limit at which battleships could operate – 20 miles – was dwarfed by the 100 mile plus range potential of the aircraft carrier. The Battle of the Coral Sea and the later Battle of Midway marked the decline of the battleship and now, sadly, the giant aircraft carriers that superceded them as kings of the sea have also been eclipsed.

Aircraft carriers came into their own in the Second World War, but the first carriers date back to 1912, when a Lieutenant C. Samson took off from a platform on the deck of the battleship Africa in a Short biplane. The feat took place when the Africa was moored off Sheerness and Lieutenant Samson used a sloping platform to get maximum lift.

Other similar experiments were tried and eventually experts developed a method of catapulting sea planes from their parent ships. This was all right for getting the planes in the air, but recovery was another matter, with the planes having to be winched aboard after landing as close to the ship as was safely possible.

This was time consuming and obviously not the answer, but it was from one such ship – the converted Isle of Man steamer Ben-My-Chree, that the first aerial torpedo attack on enemy shipping was launched. It was in the Sea of Marmara during the Dardanelles campaign, and the pilot who launched the torpedo was Flight Commander C. Edmonds.

H.M.S. Furious, a cruiser, was used for the next development. A flight deck was built onto the fore deck and Squadron Commander Dunning made the first successful landing on August 3rd, 1917, flying a Sopwith Pup. Although landing on board Furious was dangerous – the pilots had to swerve round the superstructure before they could touch down – Dunning's success led to the Navy building their first flat decked aircraft carrier.

The ship was the H.M.S. Argus, completed in 1918, and designers learned enough from its successes and failures to try for bigger, more efficient carriers such as the Ark Royal. The Ark Royal was the first of the large carriers and a formidable weapon of war. She carried 70 planes and 1,500 officers and men, and played a large part in the sinking of the Bismark; her planes crippling the pride of the German fleet by damaging her propellor, wrecking her steering gear and jamming her rudders. The Ark Royal herself was torpedoed in 1941.

Other aircraft carriers used in the war were auxiliary carriers, designed so that air cover could be given to the convoys. These were basically floating runways and were developed because the only previous method of providing air cover for the convoys was by special catapults fitted on cargo ships. Like their predecessors, these launch catapults meant that the planes – usually Sea Hurricanes – could not be recovered, and pilots were forced to ditch their planes and parachute into the sea when their fuel ran out, an understandably unpopular manoeuvre.

The first jet aircraft to land on an aircraft carrier was a De Havilland Vampire in 1946, but, ironically, it was the arrival of the jet engine, and in particular the speed and range of modern planes, that was to diminish the carriers' importance in the balance of power. Nevertheless carrier technology continued, with angled decks, steam catapults and mirror landing aids being developed, and on September 25th 1960, the world's finest carrier was launched, the U.S.S. Enterprise.

At the time the largest and most expensive American ship (180 million dollars), the Enterprise had a crew of 4,600, measured one fifth of a mile, and carried six squadrons of aircraft. A nuclear powered monster that could cruise nearly 500,000 miles without refuelling, she could launch one plane every 15 seconds.

But, technological marvel though she undoubtedly was, the Enterprise, like most other carriers, has been overtaken by the amazing technology of modern warfare, and in particular long range missiles. Helicopters are now used aboard frigates and cruisers, and there are enough nuclear submarines dotted about the globe to decimate the world's population. Like other weapons that have known death and glory, the aircraft carrier has had to take a back seat in man's relentless search for new ways to kill off his fellows.

WHAT DO YOU KNOW..

about the war ... at sea?

1. Which ship was the first casualty of The Battle of The Atlantic?
2. Where was the battleship Royal Oak sunk?
3. Was the Admiral Graf Spee:
a) A battleship
b) An aircraft carrier
c) A pocket battleship
d) A cruiser
4. Which American aircraft carrier had to be abandoned during the Battle of the Coral Sea?
5. What was a U-boat?
6. When were the Arctic Convoys started?
7. What was the purpose of the Arctic Convoys?
8. How many Japanese destroyers were assigned to the Battle of Midway?
a) 65 b) 119 c) 170
9. What was the nickname given to the commandos who paddled down the Gironde river in canoes to raid merchant shipping at Bordeaux?
10. What was an E boat?

Answers on page 61

The WAR Horse

Warfare has changed through the ages. From those prehistoric days when tribe first fought against tribe with nothing but clubs and rocks for weapons, man has seen fit to devise more and more terrible methods of destroying his brother. Today's technology has given us lunar landings, laser light shows, and computers no bigger than a fingernail, but it has also given us cruise missiles, napalm, and the H-Bomb.

It is the same with military transport. From the specialist field of the Sea Wolf and the Capturecopter, the Scorpian Tank and the Spartan Personnel carrier, despatch riders on their motorcycles and generals in their three litre staff cars, all the way down through the ranks to the ordinary soldier who was issued with his own collapsible bicycle to take with him on the D-day landings, the century since the industrial revolution has seen major upheavals in how the army moves and mobilises its forces. Faced with such a startling and diverse technical array of equipment we tend to overlook what was, for centuries, the army's only form of mobile unit – the horse.

By nature he is one of the most timid of animals and if threatened he will shy away rather than attack. His jaws are powerful, his hooves can kick fiercely, but he uses neither as weapons. To see the horse grazing quietly in some English field makes it hard to believe that less than seventy years ago horses were still in military use, carrying troops and supplies through mud, over frozen rivers, and across deserts. Patiently the horse has suffered terror and mutilation in the face of cannons and yet frequently the reward he has received for such loyalty from his masters has been cruel and forgetful.

The first recorded use of cavalry horses dates from around 900 B.C. when they begin to appear on carvings and paintings of the Scythian, Assyrian, and Median hosts who had conquered the middle Eastern Lands. Alexander the Great employed horse cavalry and chariots, so too did the ancient Greeks and the Egyptians, and later the Romans, but we must move further east, to the hordes of Mongolia, if we wish to see an army whose very fulcrum was the horse. The Mongols, under Ghengis Khan lived a nomadic life and consequently found their horses invaluable. In fact there were many more horses than men and consequently the Khan's army was able to move considerably more quickly than more conventional forces arrayed against him, for as each mount tired the rider would simply switch to a fresh horse, – this tactic enabling the Mongolians to cover as much as 120 miles in a single day. The surplus of horses also meant that should the Mongolians come up against superior forces they could try the tactical ruse of mounting dummy figures on the spare mounts in an attempt to overawe the enemy.

The training of the small, tough Mongolian horse was extremely rigorous, and almost as many horses were casualties of battle training as casualties of actual battle. For eight or ten days the horse was forced to carry around sandbags weighing as much as twenty stone. He was trotted six or seven miles each day and his rations of food and water gradually diminished. Then for a further ten days the treatment was continued, the horse's rations being further reduced although the weight on his back was gradually lightened. Finally he was given nothing at all to eat and drink for three days after which he was galloped and worked until he sweated. Then he would be unsaddled and his masters would pour buckets of ice cold water over him. Having survived such an

ordeal the Mongolians considered the horse hardy enough to be used on their raiding parties. The toughness and resilience of their horses did not however alter their masters' attitude towards them and should they go hungry on a forced march across the Steppes they thought nothing of slaughtering their horses for food.

Yet with the passage of centuries, indifference to the suffering of his horse seems to have changed very little. During the Peninsular Wars one of Von Zeithen's hussar officers simply changed horses and went about his business when the mount he was riding was badly hit in the stomach. The following day the officer happened to pass the poor beast where it lay dying. His only observation was, "I was surprised to see the horse lift its head as we rode by."

The most famous battle where massed cavalry was used as the principal assault force was, of course Waterloo. On that day, the 18th June 1815, Wellington commanded thirteen thousand horsemen, while the French, under the command of Napoleon, possessed sixteen thousand. The English cavalry on that day were succesful; – two thousand sabres galloping through a complete infantry corps, two field batteries and a cavalry brigade. The French however suffered terrible losses. Marshall Ney's five thousand cuirassiers and dragoons broke again and again on the stolid squares of allied infantry until their final shattered retreat. They left behind men and horses piled one on top of each other beneath the muzzles of the muskets and cannons. Wellington's own charger, Copenhagen, carried the

Duke unscathed through the eighteen hours of battle and earned this tribute from him: "There may have been faster horses, no doubt more handsome; but for bottom and endurance I never saw his fellow." Copenhagen was retired from military life and left to graze in peace at the duke's country seat near Reading, his most hazardous assignments now being to carry his master fox hunting.

It was the Spanish conquistadores that introduced the horse to the Americas and it was the plains Indians of North America who, though at first frightened of this strange new creature, soon learned his value. The Commanches and the Kiowas were both skilled horsemen, ranking with the Mongols as far as horsemanship, tactical prowess, and unfortunately, cruelty went. The Indian seldom groomed and never stabled his horse and when not needing him for hunting or fighting would turn him loose to fend for himself. Most of the indian 'cayuses' would have perished in the long plains winters had it not been for the squaws who left out branches of cottonwood for them to pick at. However it was the Indian's mobility at the Battle of the Little Big Horn that led to their famous victory. The U.S. cavalry, commanded by General Custer had only one survivor from that fateful day and that was a buckskin gelding who had been the mount of one Captain Myles W. Keogh and who was called, ironically enough Commanche.

Throughout the latter part of the nineteenth century and on into the twentieth century the role and usefulness of the horse as an implement of war gradually diminished. The invention of the tank and the aeroplane rendered horsemen, however skilled or courageous, an anachronism. It was left, perhaps fittingly, to the Mongolians, now part of Russia, to launch the last, full scale cavalry charge in history. It was in the November of 1941 when the might of Hitler's army were advancing on Moscow in the bitter Russian winter. Their 106th Infantry division and 107th Artillery Regiment were awaiting orders to advance when, to their astonishment, a squadron of horsemen appeared from a wood to their front and advanced at a gallop with, as one eyewitness said, "stirrup touching stirrup, riders low on their horses' necks, drawn sabres over their shoulders." At a range of one thousand yards the german guns, rifles, and automatic rifles opened up a withering fire. Of the horesemen who had started the charge only thirty reached the German positions and they

were immediately cut down by a burst of machine gun fire. The attack took only ten minutes. When it was over the two thousand horses and riders of the 44th Mongolian Cavalry Division had been cut down and lay dead or dying in the bloodstained snow. There was not a single German casualty.

It was perhaps this incident that showed that the days of the horse had gone forever from the battlefield, although some will say such a placid and loyal animal had never belonged there in the first place, for the horse has endured much for the greater glory of his masters, and endured it patiently and bravely. Consider Private John Billing's description of the horses of a gun team under enemy fire at the battle of Bull Run in the American Civil War. "A dull thud, like a pebble thrown into mud, indicated when a horse had been hit. The result of such wounds was to make the horse start for a moment or so but finally he would settle down as if it was something to be endured without making a fuss and there he would remain until struck again. I remember having my eye on one horse at the very moment when a bullet entered his neck, but the wound had no other effect on him than to make him shake his head as if pestered by a fly. Some of the horses would go down when hit by the first bullet, and after lying quiet awhile would struggle to their feet again, only to receive additional wounds. . . ."

In the stories of courage, folly, and dedication that war breeds the horse has often been forgotten. In 1954 Ronald Duncan opened the Horse of the Year show with these words: "He serves without servility; he has fought without emnity. There is nothing so powerful, nothing less violent, there is nothing so quick, nothing more patient." The history of almost all great nations owes him a debt.

Fake Fivers

During the Second World War, Hitler had a plan to flood Europe with millions of fake £5 notes, thus lessening the power of real £5 notes. Master forger Bernhard Kruger printed thousands and thousands of notes and delivered them to every European Capital. Unfortunately the war was almost over so the plan failed, but thousands of the undistributed notes were placed in water tight containers and dumped in an Austrian lake where they lay until. 1959. Then divers recovered them and the money was burned.

BROOMS &STICKS

At the beginning of the war the Local Defence Volunteers, made up mostly of men either too old or unfit for regular duty, was hit by the shortage of weapons. For weapon training they used brooms and sticks in place of rifles. One volunteer surprised everybody by arriving with an artificial leg he had borrowed.

OLD PANS WANTED

Metals were very scarce in Britain during the war and the people were often asked to turn in any old pots and pans or railings they could do without. Queen Mary, mother of George V1, was a keen supporter of this scheme, and was always looking for some useless piece of metal that could be used in the war effort. One day she returned from a country walk with what she believed was a piece of scrap metal, only to be told that it was a very important piece of a local farmers plough.

BEAR GOES TO WAR

Many fighting men adopted mascots in the war, and perhaps the strangest of all was the one adopted by the Free Folish Forces. His name was Voytek, and he was a Syrian bear. During the campaign in North Africa the soldiers made use of his strength and willingness to work by teaching him to carry shells for them. He was so likeable that the troops forgave him his occasional raids on the foods stores and after the war he was sent to Edinburgh Zoo where he lived until he was 22 years old.

GERMAN INVASION PLANS

Even though Hitler never managed to invade Britain, there was an organised resistance movement waiting for him, should he succeed. The carefully selected men were not from the armed forces, but had athletic, scientific or linguistic backgrounds. They were trained in explosives, arms and wireless operation and were then sent back to their home areas to recruit local volunteers and form them into auxiliary units of a nationwide network.

Hitler was very superstitious and had his own personal astrologer to help him plan his battle campaign. He chose the Swastika as his symbol because it had connotations of magic. He had a man dangle a pendulum over maps to help him find out where British ships were. When Churchill discovered the extent of Hitler's faith in his astrologer, he promptly sent for one himself, so he would know what kind of advice Hitler was getting.

The British people had a name for William Joyce, the traitor who broadcast German propaganda into Britain – Lord Haw Haw. His perfect English accent was mimicked in music halls and pubs and his statements were usually greeted with contempt. Lord Haw Haw was arrested after the war and brought back to England. After a highly controversial trial he was found guilty of treason and hanged in January 1946.

DEATH IN THE MOUNTAINS
THE MOUNTAINS OF SICILY...THREE BRAVE SICILIANS MAKE THEIR WAY TO A VITAL RENDEZVOUS WITH ALLIED TROOPS. THEY CARRY WITH THEM A PHIAL CONTAINING A DEADLY VIRUS DEVELOPED BY S.S. SCIENTISTS. ...LIFE IN THE MOUNTAINS IS HARD AND LONELY...
NOT FAR TO GO NOW, MARCO. WE - MARCO! NO!
ATTA-TATTA-TAT!
URRGH!
DEATH IS FINAL EVERYWHERE...
ACTION MAN AND ERNIE PERKINS HAVE BEEN ASSIGNED TO MAKE THE PICK-UP...
ATTA-TATTA-TAT!
SOUNDS LIKE TROUBLE
LET'S GO!
MINUTES LATER...
A TRAP! THEY'RE PINNED DOWN!
OPEN UP. I'LL NAIL THEM WHEN THEY TRY TO TURN.
AS ERNIE LAYS DOWN AN ACCURATE PATTERN OF FIRE ACTION MAN MAKES HIS WAY ROUND THE GERMAN'S FLANK
ERNIE'S DEADLY SHOOTING TAKES THE GERMANS BY SURPRISE...
AAARGH!
ACH! THEY ARE BEHIND US! TURN THE GUN!

AS THE GERMANS TURN THEIR BELT-FED MG-34 ON ITS HEAVY TRIPOD, ACTION MAN OPENS FIRE ...
RATTATATAT!
THE MURDEROUS CROSSFIRE EVENTUALLY TAKES ITS GRIM TOLL ...
THE PHIAL! AND IT'S UNBROKEN.
THANK GOODNESS FOR THAT. IF OUR BOFFINS DON'T COME UP WITH AN ANTIDOTE WE'RE IN TROUBLE.
NONE OF THE SICILIANS HAD SURVIVED ...
THE ARROGANT FOOLS ....THEY WILL PAY WITH THEIR LIVES...
BUT ERNIE AND ACTION MAN ARE IN TROUBLE ...
ERNIE! LOOK OUT!
ATTA-TATTA!
PTAK!
ARE YOU FIT TO TRAVEL?
I'D BETTER BE HADN'T I? THIS PLACE WILL BE SWARMING WITH GERMANS BEFORE YOU CAN SAY BOB'S YOUR UNCLE -WHICH HE IS BY THE WAY.

AFTER HASTILY DRESSING THE WOUND, THEY MAKE THEIR WAY ALONG A DESOLATE MOUNTAIN TRAIL...
ONCE WE'RE ACROSS THAT BRIDGE WE'RE SAFE
WE KNOW THAT - BUT WHAT ABOUT THE GERMANS? IF THEY'VE LAID AN AMBUSH WE...
BLIMEY! THEY'RE ON TO US!
RUN FOR IT!
A SUDDEN BURST OF FIRE CUTS SHORT ERNIE'S SPEECH...
GET GOING ERNIE I'LL BE WITH YOU IN A SECOND!
WEAVING THROUGH THE INCESSANT HAIL OF DEATH THE TWO MEN REACH THE BRIDGE...
ACH! THE FOOL WILL STRAND HIMSELF!
AS ERNIE MAKES THE OTHER SIDE, ACTION MAN DRAWS HIS DAGGER AND GETS TO WORK ON THE ROPES SUPPORTING THE BRIDGE...
BUT ACTION MAN KEEPS HOLD OF THE LAST ROPE HE CUTS...
OOOF!

SEEING ACTION MAN STRANDED AT THE BOTTOM OF THE ROPE BRIDGE, THE GERMANS OPEN FIRE ...
RATTATTATTAT!
I'M A SITTING DUCK HERE, GOT TO GET BEHIND THE BRIDGE
PKOW!
BANG!
USING THE THICK WOODEN SLATS AS A PROTECTIVE LADDER, ACTION MAN BEGINS THE LONG CLIMB UPWARDS...
INCH BY INCH ACTION MAN HAULS HIMSELF UPWARDS AS THE SPLINTERS OF WOOD AND ROCK FLY ALL ABOUT HIM...
PING!
RATTA-TATTA-TAT!
AFTER LONG, ANXIOUS MINUTES – A SWING UPWARDS FOLLOWED BY A DESPERATE SCRAMBLE...
SAFETY!
ACTION MAN AND ERNIE HEAD FOR THE COAST, LEAVING DEATH AND DESTRUCTION BEHIND THEM – BUT BRINGING THE HOPE OF LIFE TO MILLIONS OF INNOCENT PEOPLE THREATENED BY THE VIRUS.

THEY STRUCK AT NIGHT

As his flimsy two man canoe cut through the cold black waters at the mouth of the Gironde river, Major H. G. Hasler took stock of the situation. Two-thirds of his force were dead or missing and the mission had barely begun. There was still nearly sixty miles to travel along a tidal river in occupied France, and if he did manage to make it there would only be four men to carry out the intended raid on German merchant ships. What had seemed a difficult mission now looked impossible.

The story had begun some months earlier in Scotland when Major Hasler and a small commando force had undergone a special training routine that would prepare them for their very special mission. The handling of canoes was perhaps the most important part of the training but the men were run through a gruelling course of weapon training, navigation, handling high explosives, and survival at sea. Their target was the large industrial port of Bordeaux which the Germans were using as a supply port for their war effort and an occasional base for U-boats. Bombing Bordeaux would have been extremely difficult and would have cost many French lives, so it was decided to entrust the job to a handful of specially trained men.

The plan was to take the men by submarine to the mouth of the river and from there they would have to paddle the 62 miles to Bordeaux at night, hiding on the river banks during the day. The men would have to penetrate comprehensive coastal defences and evade regular river patrols before they reached their target. After the mission they were to make their escape to Spain with the help of the French Resistance.

Eleven men set out with Major Hasler in the submarine Tuna on November 12th, 1942. They had six canoes and several limpet mines to use on the ships. Almost as soon as they arrived a few miles south of the Gironde, things started to go wrong.

First of all, one of the canoes was damaged as they unloaded it through a torpedo tube. This left ten men to complete the mission, but heavy seas proved too much for some of the canoes and another four men were drowned when two of the heavily laden canoes capsized. One of the three remaining canoes disappeared as they were making their way past some moored patrol boats. With two canoes and four men, Major Hasler had to decide whether to continue.

He did not hesitate, dodging searchlights and lying quiet whenever a patrol craft approached, Major Hasler ignored the cold, the wetness and the sorrow for his comrades and led the way past the formidable defences and into the river itself. They paddled as far as they could and then went ashore to rest during the day.

For four days the four men stuck to this routine. They were spotted several times, but luckily the men and women who saw them were French and kept quiet. Eventually they reached Bordeaux.

Under the cover of darkness they crossed the river and approached a line of cargo ships moored at the quay. Their limpet mines were fused and ready to go off in nine hours. They placed two limpet mines below the waterline of one cargo ship and proceeded to give the same treatment to three others. Then at Major Hasler's signal the two canoes made off downstream. Just before dawn the two crews separated.

The danger did not end there, the second crew was captured by the Germans and shot dead. Only Major Hasler and Marine Sparks made it to Spain.

The four ships that had been mined all sank at their moorings and Major Hasler was awarded the D.S.O. and Marine Sparks the D.S.M. Their bravery and devotion to duty helped inspire the allied forces and earned them a nickname that has gone down in history – The Cockleshell Heroes.

WHAT DO YOU KNOW...

about the war ... on land?

1. What caused Britain to declare war on Germany?

2. When was war declared?

3. Did Germany fight alone in Poland?

4. What was the 'Phoney War'?

5. Who was Lord Haw Haw?

6. What was the symbol of the Dutch Resistance?

7. What was 'Operation Sealion'?

8. Where was the first Atom Bomb dropped?

9. Which young German General was sent to take charge of a small mechanised force in Africa in February 1940 and went on to military fame?

10. Which American officer was nicknamed 'Blood and Guts'?

Answers on page 61

MAGNETIC MENACE

Battles are often decided by the balance of gun against gun, man against man, tank against tank, and yet the course of war can just as easily be altered by the triumph of mind over mind. In the Second World War, scientists on both sides played cat and mouse with each other, constantly searching for new ways of breaching the enemies' defences.

In the autumn of 1939, Germany was enjoying considerable success in mining shallow waters used by British ships. British defence chiefs were especially worried because the Germans were managing to sink British ships in channels that had been cleared by minesweepers. They ordered these channels to be swept again and again and when the ships continued to sink, they knew that the Germans had successfully developed a new mine, a mine that evaded detection by conventional minesweepers.

They were understandably worried and were anxious to acquire such a mine so they could work out some form of defence against it. Their first break came in November at Shoeburyness, when two soldiers on guard duty saw a German plane release a large heavy object by parachute. The object landed in shallow water where Naval officials were able to identify it as a mine. It was seven feet long, cylindrical, and weighed 1,200 lbs.

Lieutenant Commander John Ouvry was the man in charge, and his work at the Torpedo and Mine Shore Base at Portsmouth led him to believe that the mine was magnetic, and primed to explode when large metal ships passed over it. He immediately ordered all personnel who went near the mine to remove all traces of metal from their pockets and from their clothing.

How could they examine the mine, without using metal instruments? The first thing to do was recover the detonator, and Lieutenant Commander Ouvry took this task upon himself. The morning after the mine was discovered, tracings of all external fittings to the mine were made, the measurements being relayed back to a team of men sheltering behind sandbags.

Working to these measurements, a set of non-magnetic tools were made and Lieutenant Commander Ouvry and C.P.O. Baldwin set about opening the

mine up. Their every movement was noted from behind the sandbags so that if the mine blew, the same mistakes would not be made, should the allies recover another mine. After long, anxious moments of this delicate work, Lieutenant Commander Ouvry freed the detonator from the mine's casing. It was now safe to examine the mine in full, and Lieutenant Commander Ouvry and C.P.O. Baldwin were later decorated.

Scientists had the mine moved aboard H.M.S. Vernon, where it was kept under armed guard. Patient research soon unravelled the mystery of the mines, but did nothing to suggest how the danger could be quickly and permanently eliminated. The first method, known as 'The Degaussing Girdle', was both costly and time consuming and seemed impracticable as a long term answer. 'The Degaussing Girdle' was a cable that was wound horizontally round the hull of a ship. An electric current was passed through the cable, and this neutralised the magnetism of the ships hull, allowing it to pass unharmed over the mines.

Although effective, 'The Degaussing Girdle' was not the answer, as both merchant and warships were in desperate need of an immediate counter measure. The answer finally came in the shape of some of the strangest planes to be seen in the skies over Britain. The planes were Wellingtons of the Coastal Command, but they had been fitted with a huge metal ring, some 50 feet in diameter. The ring carried a powerful electric current and when the plane flew over a mined area, the current was enough to detonate the mines.

And so the first aerial minesweeper helped clean up Britain's channels and free shipping from the magnetic menace.

WHAT DO YOU KNOW..

about the war ... in the skies?

1. How long did the Battle of Britain last?
2. How did Churchill describe the debt owed by the British people to the Battle of Britain pilots?
3. How many enemy planes were lost in the battle of Britain? Was it:
a) 1,674 b) 2,375 c) 5,921 d) 847
4. Which British pilot shot down the most enemy pilots in the Battle of Britain?
5. Who led the famous 'Dambuster's' raid?
6. Which plane was nicknamed the 'Flying Porcupine'?
7. What was a 'Doodle-Bug'?
8. Which famous fighter pilot had no legs?
9. What kind of bombers were used in the sinking of the Tirpitz?
10. Were any jets used in the Second World War?

Answers on page 61

GUERRILLA WARFARE

Action Man is on a secret mission in the steamy jungles of South East Asia. Unfortunately there are both German and Japanese troops in the area and they have the same objective as him. Can you help Action Man beat off the threat of the other soldiers and succeed?

A game for two or more players.

Players must throw a 3 or less to start, and from then on, anyone who is on a space that is landed on by another player has to go back to the start.

Players move forwards and must obey any instructions on the squares they land on.

The winner is the first player to reach the end of the trail.

SNIPER!
MISS 2 THROWS
CUTS GO SEPTIC
-MISS A THROW
ATTACKED BY HOSTILE NATIVES!
-MISS A THROW
DISCOVER ARMS CACHE
- THROW AGAIN
FIND MAP ON JAPANESE CORPSE - THROW AGAIN
BLAM!
GUN FIRES ACCIDENTALLY GIVING POSITION AWAY. -MISS A THROW
KILL A BOAR FOR FOOD - THROW AGAIN
LOSE MACHETE - GO BACK 4 SPACES
MONSOON STARTS -MISS A THROW
EXHAUSTION!
GO BACK 6 SPACES
FIND ANIMAL TRAIL - DOUBLE NEXT THROW
LOST!
MISS A THROW
ATTACKED BY A SNAKE!
MISS A THROW
END

DEATH PATROL

Throughout December 1941, the Imperial Japanese Army had been smashing their way South through Manila. Moving south from Kota Baru and Besut on the South China Sea, they had passed Kuala Lipis, Seremban, Gemas and Malacca, and by the end of January they had almost reached Singapore itself. The British Army was on the run, and Action Man was sent in to help organise the lone bands of brave soldiers still desperately trying to stall the relentless progress of the rampaging Sons of Nippon.

As the Lancaster's engines throbbed noisily, the battle-hardened veteran checked his parachute and prepared to jump. He had hitched a lift with a lone bomber sent to try and cut the supply lines. 'Biffo' Hodgkinson came and stood by him, gazing down at the lush vegetation passing quickly below.

"They're in there, somewhere, Action Man." He said, shaking his head slowly and fingering the long scar on his chin. "But that's a pretty big jungle to get lost in." He offered his hand.

Action Man did not answer. He took Biffo's hand, shook it quickly, and jumped. Biffo watched the 'chute billow open as Action Man passed out of sight.

"Good luck," he said quietly, "You're going to need it."

As he dropped out of the sky, Action Man studied the vast expanse of greenery below. The jungle was a cruel and ruthless enemy that took no sides.

On his way down, he surveyed the tree tops for any sign of life, any inkling that under that seemingly impenetrable barrier of green, Colonel Straker was waiting with his men.

Straker was the last of the senior officers in the jungle. He was trying to get all the stragglers to meet at certain secret co-ordinates that had been broadcast in code over the last three days. The idea was to get together a big enough force to smash their way through the Japanese front line and reach Singapore.

Action Man's thoughts were rudely interrupted by the sight of the treetops rushing up to meet him. With his legs close together and his hands above his head clinging to the straps of his parachute, Action Man plunged through the upper branches of the trees and then felt the sharp tug of the straps. His parachute had snagged in the tree tops. He pulled his dagger and snapped one of his straps and was about to cut the other when noises in the jungle below made him hesitate. Still Swinging precariously he took out two grenades and held them close to his mouth, ready to pull the pins out with his teeth.

He hoped it was a wild boar or a monkey, but he was out of luck. It was a boy, not more than sixteen, walking clumsily, watching warily, and carrying a double barrelled shot gun. Action Man put his grenades back on his belt and placed his dagger by the last remaining strap holding him to the tree.

The boy seemed frightened, but of whom? He wasn't Japanese, but that was no guarantee that his loyalties were with the allied forces. He made his way cautiously along the edge of a narrow animal trail, and when he was directly below him, Action Man cut the last strap.

Action Man dropped like a stone, landing square in the middle of the boy's back, knocking him flat to the floor. The shotgun flew from his grasp, hit a gnarled Banyan tree and went off, showering the empty jungle with buckshot.

Although badly winded, the boy was soon on his feet, wriggling and scratching for his life. A sharp slap from Action Man's hand, coupled with an iron grip on the boy's shoulder, soon made him stop.

"Do you speak English?" asked Action Man, holding the youth at arm's length.

"Yes, yes I do," said the boy, "my name is John Carmelo and I work on a rubber estate and –"

"Then come with me," said Action Man. "That blast is bound to bring any Japanese that might be in the area."

He picked up the boy's shotgun, grimaced at its neglected condition and led the way into the thick jungle. The boy followed meekly. After ten minutes they stopped. Action Man held up the boy's shotgun.

"John, the first chance we get, I want you to clean that gun. A badly maintained weapon is as dangerous to the owner as to the enemy. We're in for a tough time in the near future and if you can't act like a good soldier you might as well surrender and –"

Action Man was cut off by the sound of gunfire, less than one hundred yards away. He thrust the weapon back in the youngster's hands.

"Load it as we go along. Stay close, don't make a sound, and don't do anything until I tell you!"

They made their way cautiously towards the sound of gunfire. Through a gap in the foliage, Action Man saw a group of Japanese soldiers firing into the undergrowth. He put his hand lightly on John's shoulder.

"Follow me. Don't fire that gun unless you have to."

John nodded nervously as Action Man counted out five ammunition clips for his sten. He put two in his pocket, one in each hand and quickly replaced the one already in his gun. Without speaking, Action Man edged close to the Japanese. He could see four of them but from the sounds of fighting there were many more, grouped in a semicircle round their prey. He stopped momentarily by a tree and then sprayed the Japanese soldiers with all 32 rounds of his first clip. He ran swiftly to new cover, re-loading as he did so. With a brief

glance to check John was still with him, Action Man opened up again, expending all 32 bullets in one burst before running on.

He reloaded again behind some undergrowth and let off another burst, beginning to run as soon as it had finished. He continued this way with an awed John in tow until they reached the target of the Japanese guns, seven English soldiers fighting for their lives. Action Man jumped down beside a corporal with a Lee Enfield.

"How are you for ammo?" He asked. The corporal shrugged.

"Not bad, but we were outnumbered until you came along. How many have you got with you?"

Action Man didn't answer. He rose to his feet and emptied yet another clip full of bullets into the area where the fiercest shooting was coming from. He dropped back to his knees and looked closer at the corporal who was looking at John's shotgun with a baffled expression on his face.

"Do you know where Straker is?" He asked. The corporal snorted.

"Captured – two days ago. There's not many of us left." He looked ruefully towards the Japanese positions. "Do you suppose they're playing dead over there?"

Action Man put another clip in his Sten and raked the jungle. There was a scream of pain and then the sound of soldiers retreating. He almost smiled. So his trick to make them think they were outnumbered had worked.

After half an hour's waiting in complete silence, Action Man went forward to discover if the Japanese soldiers really had retreated or were playing possum. He passed over seven dead soldiers before he heard a groan. He moved quickly to find a Japanese soldier with a bad wound in his shoulder, lying on the ground and trying desperately to stretch his injured arm towards a Nambu model 14 pistol lying just out of his reach. Action Man kicked the gun away, turned him on his back and searched him.

He was surprised by the number of documents the soldier carried. He propped him up against a tree and did his best to tend to his wound, pumping him with questions all the time. The Japanese gave nothing away.

By this time the rest of the surviving English soldiers had come forward, accompanied by John Carmelo. The corporal was the first to speak.

"What should we do with him?"

"Kill him?" asked one of the privates. Action Man finished bandaging the wounded soldier's shoulder.

"He's coming with us," he said simply, "he's carrying a lot of papers that might be important."

"He'll slow us up." said a voice. Action

Man stared at the assembled soldiers, and his eyes were cold.

"He's coming with us."

The weary band headed south, steering clear of the main trails. The corporal had told Action Man that he thought all captured soldiers had been taken south to be used as workers strengthening the supply lines to the Japanese front.

They travelled all afternoon without stopping. The only sounds were the brushing of leaves, the breaking of branches, the swish of the machettes and their own heavy breathing. At the front of the party Action Man noticed that all the sounds were getting louder. Fatigue was beginning to tell, and the clumsier they became – the easier they would be to detect He turned to order a halt when the man next to him fell to the ground with the sound of a single gunshot. Action Man riddled the sniper's position with gunfire. A short cry, then a Japanese sniper fell with a dull thud to the floor.

"We're getting closer," said Action Man after gathering the dead soldier's possessions. "Watch out for bamboo bombs."

Bamboo bombs were vicious balls of bamboo leaves covered with wire and packed with high explosives and sharp bamboo splinters. To tread on one meant certain death.

They marched forward again. After another hour without incident, Action Man found a suitable spot to bed down for the night. The Japanese prisoner looked ready to drop and John Carmelo was sweating and shivering at the same time.

After a cold meal washed down with hot strong coffee the men lay down and slept. Action Man and Corporal Jones took first watch. They heard nothing except the scurrying of the many nocturnal animals in the jungle. At two hundred hours they woke the men that were to relieve them.

One of these men was Private Noddy Smith. A brave, stubborn man, Noddy had been wandering the jungles for almost four weeks two of them without ammunition, covering hundreds of miles and killing six Japanese soldiers. He would not admit it to anyone, but the limits of his physical endurance had been met. He was tired, dog tired, and soon after he took his post, the lids to his eyes began slowly to droop.

The Japanese prisoner had been biding his time. He had recognised Action Man as his most dangerous adversary, and when the big man had settled himself down he decided to act. He knew he had little chance of escape, but at least he could go down fighting and end the terrible pain in his shoulder. Next to him, John Carmelo was shivering uncontrollably, his shotgun resting butt upwards against a tree. He slid slowly forward and grabbed the weapon.

Action Man was awakened by a triumphant cry to see the Japanese prisoner holding Carmelo's shotgun and pointing it directly at him. He slipped the catch on his bren and turned to fire, but it was too late.

BKOOM!

"Aaaaiiuurgh!"

As the Japanese soldier fired both barrels, the force of the blast met the thick mud that caked the insides, blocking them both completely. In a second the barrels split open and peeled back, and the man holding the gun fell instantly to the ground, stone dead. Action Man went over and retrieved the blood covered stock of the shotgun. John Camelo was looking up with a mixture of bewilderment and fear. Action Man held the stock close.

"I thought I told you to clean this thing," he said grimly.

Fearing the sounds would alert any Japanese troops in the area, they moved out again in almost total darkness. Progress was slow and noisy, but they met no further trouble. As dawn was breaking they were looking down from a small hill on a sight that made Action Man smile coldly.

Under the watchful eyes of the Japanese, about two hundred British soldiers and half that number of natives were clearing a strip of jungle to make an emergency airfield. There was a cluster of wooden buildings with six large trucks standing idle nearby. Across the other side of the proposed airfield, several Japanese soldiers stood by a train on a single line. Action Man could not help but admire the speed with which the Japanese had organised themselves though he despised the methods they used to do so. He spoke quietly to the men.

"I want three of you to get as close to that work party as possible and pick out your targets before you fire. The rest of you will come with me to knock out those trucks and come in on the Japanese from the flank. If that chain gang joins in, we should have a chance."

Three men melted into the undergrowth and Action Man handed out some pencil-time fuses to drop in the trucks' petrol tanks. He looked into the faces of his men and noted with satisfaction that the tiredness had been replaced by tense, nervous energy. He turned and began to lead them down the hill.

About two hundred yards from the trucks they stopped. The jungle had ended suddenly and there was no cover. They would have to rush it.

"Keep low and move fast. As soon as we're spotted – open up!"

They ran at a crouch across the flat ground that separated them from the trucks. They made half the distance before the nearest bunch of Japanese soldiers saw them and reached for their weapons. Still running, Action Man emptied a full clip in their direction, and slipped another into his sten without breaking stride.

At the sound of Action Man's party's assault, the three others assigned to the work party began shooting. They had singled out the guards and taken a certain number each, to eliminate the possibility of all of them wasting bullets at the same target.

Action Man was nearing the trucks. The Japanese had recovered well and were hitting them with everything they had, and even now, more and more soldiers were pouring out of the wooden buildings. Action Man mowed down two soldiers standing on the back of the nearest truck, took a pencil time fuse from his belt, unscrewed the truck's petrol cap and dropped it in. As he ran to the second truck he saw more of his men further along, also slipping pencil bombs into fuel tanks. They were fighting well, but unless the captured soldiers turned on their captors and joined them they would have no chance.

Action Man signalled his men to fight their way past the wooden buildings. They did not want to be close to the trucks when they blew. He pressed himself close to the side of the truck, pulled the pins on two grenades and threw them at the nearest Japanese soldiers. Even as they exploded he was throwing two more. He rushed forward towards the buildings, firing as he ran.

Across the clearing the three soldiers sent out to eliminate the working party guards had done their job well. Five had died within the first six shots and the remainder had either fled to cover or were fighting for their lives against the prisoners. Although weak through overwork, the soldiers and natives who had been taken prisoner grasped their chance of freedom like a drowning man grasps a lifebelt. They fought like furies, rushing unarmed at the Japanese guns with a ferocity that surprised even the Japanese themselves.

The first truck blew and was followed

quickly by the others. Black fumes wafted slowly across the compound as the battle raged even stronger. Action Man was sprinting across the makeshift airfield towards the train.

The Japanese at the train put up stiff resistance, but not stiff enough. The British soldiers, backed by a swarm of yelling prisoners, were not to be denied. After four minutes it was over, and Action Man was studying the train's controls as the prisoners boarded the trucks behind. An urgent voice made him look up.

"Action Man! Colonel Straker's here."

Action Man looked down from the cab to see Private Noddy Smith with a thin man in Khaki shorts. The bruises on his body and thick red welts across his neck and face told Action Man that Colonel Straker had had a hard time. Straker leapt nimbly into the cab, trying hard not to wince and holding his ribs very carefully.

"Action Man – glad to see you. You've done a fine job." he said.

Action Man stared into the Colonel's troubled but defiant eyes. The Colonel continued.

"The Japanese cracked our code. They nabbed us and then they nabbed everyone else coming to rendezvous with us. We're all glad you came along." He slapped Action Man on the back. "Now what are we going to do about getting out of here?"

Action Man smiled at the Colonel's renewed enthusiam.

"I thought we might take this train as far as it will go." He said simply.

He leaned out of the cab to check that everyone was in the trucks, returned a nervous wave from John Carmelo, and started the train. Within minutes they were speeding down the track.

"There's a bridge near the Japanese front line," said Colonel Straker, shovelling coal into the train's boiler, "I don't know if the Japanese have taken it yet, but if they haven't I'm sure our chaps will have blown it up by now."

Action Man produced a map and the two men studied it.

"There," said Straker, pointing at the creased paper, "there it is."

Action Man studied the coordinates.

"We should be there in twenty minutes. I'll stop her before we reach it."

"Better be careful about Japanese soldiers on our trail. When they find out about this, they'll be sending another train in pursuit."

"Action Man! Village ahead!"

Action Man thrust his head out of the speeding cab. It wasn't a village as such, just a couple of buildings and a water tower. What made it interesting was that there were Japanese soldiers with machine guns on almost every vantage point. Action Man put the train at full throttle. He leaned out of one side with his sten at the ready while Noddy Smith and the Colonel took the other. Behind them, he knew that every armed man would be at the ready.

The Japanese started firing as soon as the train was in range. Action Man replied in kind. Bullets rained down upon them, some of them puncturing the boiler of the racing, hurrying, train. If only they could make it through the ambush. He saw Straker throw a grenade. He raked the top of the water tower and one Japanese soldier made the long fall to earth. Behind him he could hear cheering and sporadic shooting.

Suddenly they were through and the village was disappearing behind them.

Action Man studied the train's controls with a frown.

"She's losing steam." He said, "We'd better get off."

He slowed the engine to a halt and Colonel Straker stepped off the running

plate. The men they had rescued clambered out of the trucks, many of them armed with guns they had stolen from dead Japanese at the airstrip. Colonel Straker held up his hand for silence and then spoke.

"It's the last lap, now lads." He said. "It'll be tough but I for one am glad we've got the chance to make it. This time there's no turning back."

As the men cheered Action Man put the train in reverse, and locked the lever at full steam. He jumped down as the train started chugging backward and looked around him. More than two hundred ragged, cheering men looked back. He smiled as he saw young John Carmelo busily cleaning a captured Japanese gun. He saw hope, determination and courage on the faces of the once captured men. Win or lose, for them this was the last lap, the last chance for freedom. For him . . .? He fitted yet another clip to his sten.

"Let's go!"

The Chindits

By 1942, the end of the war looked a long way away and the long years of bitter fighting on all fronts was the gloomy prospect for the allied forces. One glimmer of light in these dark days, however, appeared with the development of some long range penetration groups who were to prove among the most heroic fighting forces of the war – the Chindits.

The Chindits were formed by Orde Wingate who took the name from the Chinthe, a mythical beast that was half lion and half eagle. Wingate thought the animal was an apt symbol for a force that was going to need close ground to air co-operation if it was to succeed.

At that stage of the war General Mutagachi, Commander of the Japanese 15th Army, regarded the Chindwin River as a secure barrier behind which his troops would be safe from attack on the ground. Wingate's plan was to cross the Chindwin and use the Chindits in guerilla operations against Japanese communications and outposts. He thought that a force the size of a brigade would be the most suitable – big enough to strike with real force, but small enough to evade capture. The 77th Indian Brigade was re-organised and the soldiers, now Chindits, were given special training in jungle survival and all aspects of guerrilla warfare, especially demolition and radio communication. Behind enemy lines they would be supplied by the R.A.F. and would use pack animals to carry their equipment.

On February 14th, 1943, the first Chindit operation behind the Japanese lines began when two groups – a Northern Group with 2,200 men and 850 mules, and a southern group of 1,000 men and 250 mules – crossed the Chindwin River under cover of darkness while regular forces created a diversionary action. Moving eastward the northern group split into five columns, and the southern group into two. The different forces carried out attacks on Japanese vehicles, outposts, and troops. They blew up bridges and cut railway lines and by March they had crossed the Irawaddy, a hundred miles east of the Chindwin.

But the Japanese had been quick to learn, and when they recognised the magnitude of the Chindit threat they deployed two of their five divisions in Burma to deal with it. The Chindits were forced to withdraw and by mid-April they were back in India, missing one third of their men and most of their equipment.

Although the operation was not an outstanding success, the Chindits caused the Japanese enough problems to make the previously sceptical Chiefs of Staff agree with Wingate that the potential was there, and that with the facts they had learned from the first operation, they would be more able to exploit them in the future. The force was increased from two Brigades to six, Wingate was promoted to major-general and was given the No.1 Air Commando – a force equivalent to eleven squadrons, to work with. The Chindits also had a new role. The plan was for the Chindits to be sent into enemy territory miles ahead of the main army, establish various strongholds and then fight it out with the enemy until the main army arrived. By March, 1944, using gliders to transport some troops and sending others on foot, the Chindits had 9,000 men deep behind enemy lines.

The Chindits fought from March, well into the autumn: The Japanese had been caught by surprise once again, and once again they reacted speedily and efficiently, their airforce destroying most of the Chindits air cover and a force under General Hayashi being sent to meet them on the ground. The fighting was fierce and the Chindits acquitted themselves as a force of uncommon bravery and skill. Even when Wingate was killed after his plane crashed in the jungle, the Chindits did not lose heart, and their mission to fight their way north to meet up with General Stilwell's advance from China was tackled with their usual tenacity. They took Mogaung, although Stilwell's advance on Myitkyina ended in failure.

In autumn, the exhausted Chindits were replaced by the 36th Indian/British Division. Without the support of the main army, Wingate's bold plan to use the Chindits as a permanent spearhead had failed, but the courage of his men paid tribute to his brave ideas.

Men of Courage

Courage comes in many forms, but the Second World War threw up several examples of bravery so great it inspires awe and thankfulness to this very day. Jean Moulin, and Witold Pilecki, showed just that kind of courage.

Jean Moulin was a Frenchman who joined the Resistance at the start of the war. The average lifespan of a Resistance leader in France under the Germans was about six months, but Moulin worked tirelessly and bravely for years. He was particularly successful at unifying the various Resistance groups and stopping the kind of inter-group fighting that had weakened the underground movements in Yugoslavia and Poland.

But Moulin's luck eventually ran out when he was captured by the Germans and subjected to some horrific tortures. He never said a word. After several days continuous beating he was unable to speak, but when he signalled that he would like a pencil and a piece of paper, his torturers thought they had cracked him at last. They gave him the pencil and paper, but instead of writing down secrets, Moulin calmly drew a cruelly accurate cartoon of his chief torturer and handed the pencil back. He died soon after.

If Moulin's spirit and durability were astounding, so were the exploits of Witold Pilecki, a Pole. Pilecki deliberately got arrested by the Germans so he could be sent to Auschwitz, where he intended to start a Resistance movement.

Pilecki was sent to Auschwitz and helped start some kind of movement before he escaped and went back to Poland just in time for the Warsaw uprising. He survived that ill-fated revolt and escaped from Poland and made his way to Italy. After the Russians took over Poland, Pilecki returned on a mission for the exiled Polish Government in London. This time, however, his luck ran out and he was captured and shot.

The incredible bravery of these two men is an inspiration to us all.

CROSSWAR

This crossword is especially designed to test your knowledge of the Second World War. All the answers are places that saw action. If you find the clues too hard, try unscrambling the answers from the list on the opposite page.

Clues Across.

1. One of the Islands seen by the Americans as a vital base for the air bombardment of Japan. Scene of terrible bloodshed that resulted in only 200 of the 25,000 Japanese defending it being taken prisoner and more than 26,000 U.S. Marines losing their lives.

3. The fight for this city marked the end of Germany's advance into Russia with some of the most gruelling and sustained fighting of the war. Hitler finally abandoned his army to the Russians, and the defeat had a bad effect on German morale.

6. Home of a very famous road that was a lifeline for the Chinese in their war with Japan. The road was bombed so often that the Chinese were constantly working to repair it. They consoled themselves with the knowledge that it cost the Japanese £250 for each crater and themselves only 2p to fill it in.

7. Scene of the allies re-entry into Europe in 1943 when Hitler and Mussolini were still trying to save face in Africa. leaving this island open to attack.

11. Horror came to this city in the shape of an atom bomb. The Americans dropped their second atom bomb here, virtually ending the war.

12. One of the Marianas islands that had an airstrip. Fierce air and sea fighting emphasised the importance of this island to Japan's inner ring of defence.

13. Scene of an unprovoked Japanese air raid that brought America into the war.

16. European city attacked in the early hours of May 10th by the German army, using tanks and parachutists in a famous victory for Hitler.

17. Baltic state invaded by Stalin in June 1940, who saw it as a buffer against Hitler's forces.

Clues Down.

2. The scene of three historic battles and probably the most famous city of the war in Africa.

4. Famous beach head where British and American forces began the invasion of Italy that finally led to the capture of Rome.

5. Huge country eventually invaded by Japan.

6. The Battle of the -----, lasting from 16th December 1944 to the 24th December has been the subject of numerous books and a famous feature film.

8. Hosted famous conference in 1944 when the threat of Japan was discussed by world leaders.

9. Egyptian town that Rommel failed to reach. Home of 1943 Anglo-American conference.

10. Town on the 'toe' of Italy that was used as a landing place by General Miles Dempsey's 13th Corps, under cover of bombardment from Sicily.

14. Capital of Italy, finally reached by the Fifth Army on June 4th, 1944.
15. Line from Pisa through Florence where the Germans checked the allied advance in Italy.

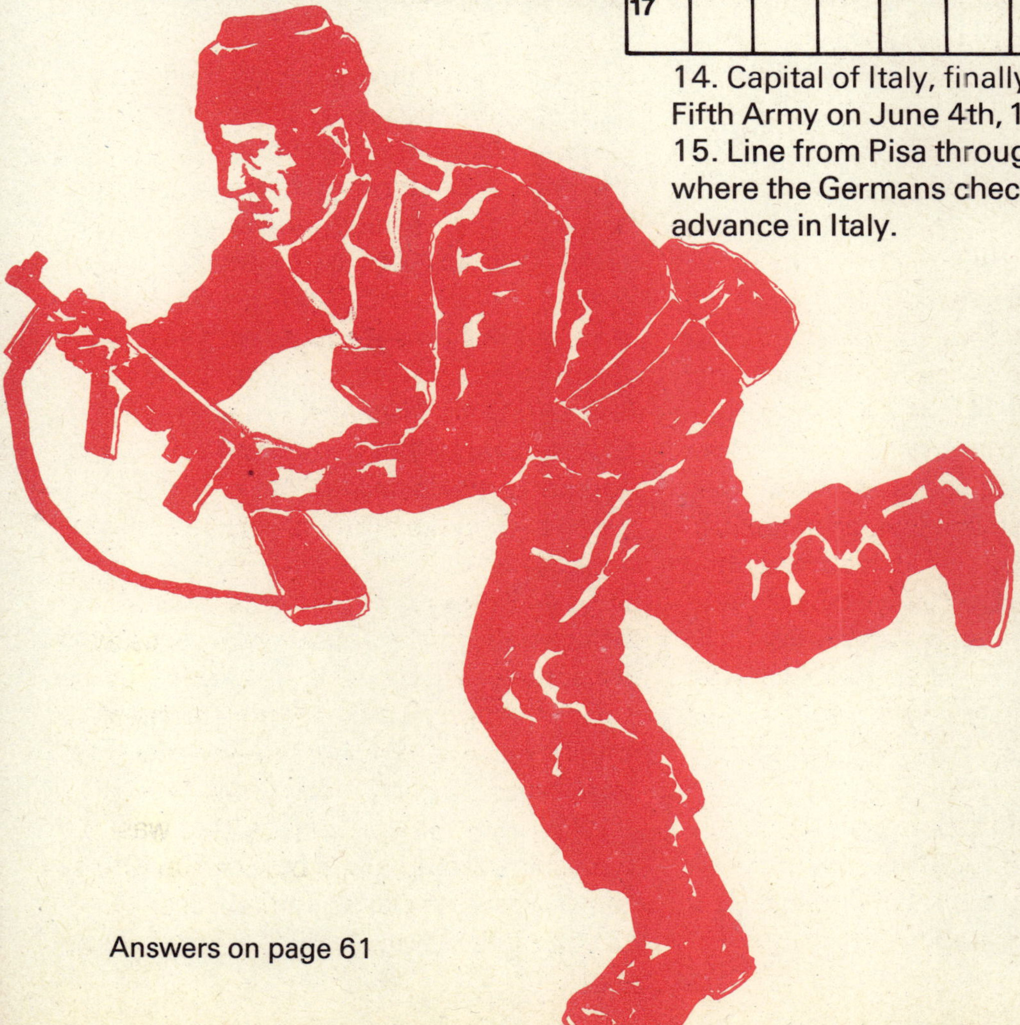

RUMBA
GRANISLAID
ROICA
MAGU
ATALY
GLEBU
LAPER ROARHUB
MATTERROD
IANOTSE
ANIKASAG
ROAN
MORE
OGREGI
DAINI
ZANIO
ICIYSL
WOI MAIJ
ANEMILA

Answers on page 61

RAID ON THE ROCKETS

In the Spring of nineteen forty five Germany was in ruins. Along her eastern frontiers the Russian army advanced ferociously further forward every day, while from the south and west British and American forces pushed deeper and deeper into the heart of the Third Reich. Her army was ill equipped and undermanned, her rulers frightened, her soldiers dispirited. Yet still she fought on. The country's grain and potato harvests were commandeered by the army and turned into alcohol while the civilian population went hungry. And the alcohol was taken North by train to the flat marshy shores of the Baltic; to Peenemunde and the rocket bases. It was from there that the Nazis launched their last, and perhaps most sinister weapons;– the V1 and the V2 rockets. Fired indiscriminately at a defenceless London, they sped unmanned across the North Sea to their unknown targets, carrying their payload of death. Action Man and his fellow commando Tom Stone were sent on a dangerous mission.

"Take a look at that, Action Man," said the Captain of the submarine and offered his passenger the viewfinder on the periscope. Action Man swivelled the handles of the periscope slightly until the bright yellow and orange tail of a rocket could be seen disappearing into the night sky. Then his eyes returned to his immediate objective. The long low lying hangars and huts of the rocket base were outlined against the low horizon. In the foreground, across a half mile of open water, were the lagoons and brackish waters of the river mouth, surrounded by sandbars and banks of reeds. Set on one of the sandbars and surrounded by barbed wire was a tower. From the top of the tower a searchlight beam played to and fro along the coastline. "This is as close as I can go, Action Man," said the Captain.

"That's fine," said Action Man, "I'll go and check with Tom Stone and see if all our equipment is ready."

"Right you are. We surface in five

minutes."

"We'll be ready," said Action Man.

Tom Stone, the commando, was crouched in the space below the forward hatch. He grinned at Action Man as he approached. "We go in five minutes, is everything ready?"

"Everything's ready," said Stone quickly checking the mechanism on his Heckler and Koch sub machine gun.

"You remember the drill?" Action Man asked his companion.

"The light in the tower moves along the shoreline once every three minutes said Stone, "That gives us twenty minutes to row ashore but less than three when we're in range of the light."

"Right."

"We hide the dinghy in the reeds and then take the tower."

"Right. We hide the dinghy on the east of the tower. Once it's taken then you wait there and operate the searchlight as if nothing's wrong. That gives us another half hour until the R.A.F. plane flies over. The plane will drop a special mission pod on one of the sandbars to the west of the tower. As soon as you hear the plane overhead then you're to sound the alarm and train the searchlight on the dinghy that we've left in the reeds to the east. Then make your way westward to the rendezvous position at the pod."

Outside the submarine, the water could be heard hissing off its' iron sides as it slowly surfaced. The hatch slid open and both Action Man and Tom Stone donned their back packs and between them lifted the already inflated dinghy onto the sub's deck.

"Good luck," whispered the captain as the two men climbed into the frail craft.

"Thanks captain," said Action Man, "We'll see you again in a couple of hours."

"I hope so," murmured the naval officer as he watched the dinghy disappear over the dark water.

In the dinghy the two men paddled in silence; the only sound being the whisper of their paddles in the still sea. Finally, with the shoreline one hundred yards away Action Man looked at his watch. "Okay, Tom," he whispered, "We're in range of the searchlight now, let's start the three minute dash." The paddles began to bite strongly into the icy water and the dinghy moved more quickly towards the shore. In front of him Action Man heard Stone counting off the seconds, "thirty five, thirty six, thirty seven, thirty eight . . . ."

"The light's coming back again, Tom, keep paddling."

The reeds were much closer now and a pair of water fowl, disturbed at their

approach fluttered up into the air. Stone was still counting. "Ninety eight, ninety nine, one hundred, one hundred and one, one hundred and . . . . . ." The dinghy brushed into the reeds and Action Man leaped into the shallow muddy water and grabbing the anchor rope began to pull it towards where they grew the densest. In the dinghy Tom Stone was now lying flat, his Heckler and Koch cradled in his hands. "One hundred and twenty eight, one hundred and twenty nine," his voice continued to count off the seconds. Action Man pulled the dinghy further into the reeds, bending some of the taller ones over to conceal it. The light grew closer. "One hundred and seventy two, one hundred and seventy three," murmured Stone in the same even voice.

"Get down, Tom," whispered Action Man. Moments later the searchlight passed across their hiding place in the reeds.

"Nice going, five seconds to spare," whispered Tom.

"Right," said Action Man, "Let's take the tower."

The two men ran across the dark sandbar in a low crouch. Reaching the barbed wire they dropped flat in the sand. Stone took a pair of wire cutters from his belt and went to cut the wire.

"Don't Tom," whispered Action Man grasping his friend's arm, "it's electrified."

Instead he took the small shovel that was strapped to his back pack and tunnelled quickly through the soft sand. He wriggled through and pulled Tom Stone after him. The two men reached the base of the tower and began to climb slowly and silently. Above them they could hear the voices of the two sentries chatting quietly to one another. Reaching the tower's vantage point they paused for a moment, then, working with the ruthless efficiency that their commando training had instilled in them, the two men sprang quickly into action. The sentries were soon overpowered and lay unconscious at their feet. "Here," said Action Man, taking one of their helmets, "Put this on instead of your beret. If a patrol comes past then they'll be less likely to recognise you." Then he fastened one end of his rope to the parapet and let it snake down to the ground. "I'll leave the rope here, it'll help you get away more quickly once you've set off the alarm."

"Okay, Action Man," said Tom, "You're on your own from here."

"Don't forget, Tom, sound the alarm when you hear the R.A.F. plane overhead." Action Man nodded farewell to his companion and then slid quickly down the rope and onto the sand. He waded across a shallow lagoon and then crawled through the icy water and reeds. Suddenly he heard

voices directly in front of him and froze. A flashlight danced across the flat countryside. It was a German patrol. Peering into the darkness he made out the distinctive uniform of the stormtroopers. Action Man lay still, hardly breathing until they had passed. If the patrol had passed so close then he must be near to the road, he thought.

Sure enough, moving forward he found himself on the edge of the road that led toward the rocket base's main gates. He moved along it quietly, crouching low and travelling in the shadows of the muddy ditch. Soon he came within sight of the main gates. On either side was a sentry box and in both boxes sat a sentry with a Schmeisser machine gun. Now he had to wait for the aeroplane.

He heard the drone of its approach before either of the guards and moved still closer to their position. Presently one of the guards heard it and walked across to his companion and said something to him. The two men peered up into the sky as the sound of the aeroplane grew closer. As the sound grew louder the two men seemed to get more excited, more worried. Any minute now, thought Action Man, waiting for Tom Stone to sound the alarm in the tower.

Suddenly the siren blared and the searchlight in the tower span round to where they had hidden the dinghy in the reeds. The two guards shouted to one another and then began to run toward the point that the searchlight indicated. As

they did so Action Man slipped silently through the entry gate and dashed for the shadows to the side of the bunkhouse. Stormtroopers were spilling from its lighted entrance donning uniforms and clutching weapons. Some were taking their Lugers from their holsters, others unfolding the stocks on their Schmeissers. Action Man pressed further back into the shadows as they hurriedly formed into ranks and then marched down to the gates and looked out to where the first two guards had now reached the concealed dinghy. They beckoned their fellow stormtroopers over to witness their discovery.

Action Man glanced around the rocket base until he located the large rocket hangar. R.A.F. recconaissance had done a good job, he thought, remembering the aerial photographs he had been shown at the mission briefing. He took his pack off his back and set the demolition charge to explode in five minutes, then, with Sten gun at the ready, dashed from hut to hut until he was standing at the base of the great corrugated iron hangar. In the large sliding door was set a smaller personnel door with a light bulb burning above it. He reached up with the butt of his Sten and smashed the light and then rapped sharply on the door. A fat man in an unbuttoned tunic answered his summons and while he was still looking at Action Man in surprise the commando dived on top of him and dealt him two fierce punches. The man sighed and sank to the floor while Action Man quickly closed the small door behind him.

Inside the hangar was dimly lit. Action Man could make out the gleaming fuselages to about thirty rockets. He ran quickly to the first one and lay a dummy charge beside it. Should his entry to the rocket base be discovered then perhaps finding a dummy charge would prevent the Germans from locating the real one. This he left much more intricately concealed amongst the rows of dials, gauges, and pipes that were used in the assembly of the V2 rockets. Then with the charge set he peered once more through the crack in the door. Most of the personnel on the base were now gathered close to the main gates and peering into the darkness where the sentries and the guards had uncovered the dinghy that he had left to the east of the watch-tower. He took his wirecutters from his pack and ran to the perimeter fence about two hundred yards to the west of the main gate. Now came the big gamble. Was this fence electrified like the one around the tower? With only three and a half minutes left before the charges detonated he didn't have much chance to think it over. He kicked out at the fence. No reaction. He put the wirecutters to the fence and pressed down on their handles. The wires parted and whistled back into the darkness and

Action Man, thankful for his luck, hurried through the gap and out to the countryside that surrounded the base.

He ran steadily westward toward the shore, toward the point where he was to meet Tom Stone. As he ran he counted off the seconds until the charge was detonated. Would Tom have found the special mission pod that the plane had dropped for them? If he hadn't then things were going to get pretty hot here. He splashed through the last shallow lagoon and then ran along the sandbar to where he expected Tom to be waiting for him.

He was almost on top of his companion before he saw him. "Action Man," called Tom, "The pod's landed over here."

The commando had just detached the pod from its billowing silk parachute. Action Man threw some sand on it to stop it blowing away and attracting attention. As he did so Stone pulled the two locking rings to separate the two halves of the pod. Working as a team the two men unfolded the dinghy that it contained. "Okay Tom, you inflate the dinghy while I set up the Bren gun."

Action Man reached into the pod and brought out the light machine gun. "How did it go?" asked Stone as Action Man set the gun on its tripod.

"The diversion you set up worked fine," replied Action Man, "as for the charges I laid we'll find out in seven seconds."

The two men waited in silence, counting down to zero as their commando training had taught them to do. Suddenly a great flash of light broke across the sky and then a rumbling shockwave reached them. "It seems we were successful," said Action Man grinning back at the flaming wreckage of the rocket hangar, "Now to take out that light." He aimed along the sights of the bren gun and fired a short, accurate burst toward the top of the look out tower. The glass cover exploded into fragments and the light went out. Now all that lit the scene were the crisscrossing torches of the stormtroopers and the flickering flames from the rocket base.

"Let's go," said Tom Stone, "pushing the dinghy into the sea, "the submarine will be waiting for us."

"Yeah," agreed Action Man, "I'm looking forward to that."

"You must be," said Stone, "You deserve a rest."

"It's not a rest I'm looking forward to," said Action Man.

"Then what is it?" asked his friend puzzled as they paddled out toward their rendezvous point with the sub.

"The next assignment."

ANSWERS

CROSSWAR

Clues across:
1. Iwo Jima
3. Stalingrad
6. Burma
7. Sicily
11. Nagasaki
12. Guam
13. Pearl Harbour
16. Rotterdam
17. Estonia

Clues down:
2. Alamein
4. Anzio
5. India
6. Bulge
8. Yalta
9. Cairo
10. Reggio
14. Rome
15. Arno

WHAT DO YOU KNOW ABOUT THE WAR . . . AT SEA?

1. The Athenia sank the day war was declared.
2. Scapa Flow.
3. c).
4. U.S.S. Lexington.
5. A German submarine.
6. September 1941.
7. To get supplies to Russia.
8. a).
9. The Cockleshell Heroes.
10. The German equivalent of a British M.T.B.

WHAT DO YOU KNOW ABOUT THE WAR? . . . ON LAND?

1. The German invasion of Poland.
2. Sunday, September 3rd, 1939.
3. No, Russia fought with them.
4. The period between the invasion of Poland and Hitler's Western offensive the following spring.
5. William Joyce.
6. An orange V.
7. Hitler's plan to invade Britain.
8. Hiroshima.
9. Rommel.
10. Patton.

WHAT DO YOU KNOW ABOUT THE WAR . . . IN THE SKIES?

1. 84 days.
2. 'Never in the field of human conflict was so much owed by so many to so few.'
3. b).
4. James Edgar 'Johnny' Johnson.
5. Gut Gibson.
6. The Shorts Sunderland Flying Boat.
7. A flying bomb.
8. Douglas Bader.
9. The Avro Lancaster.
10. Yes, at the end the Germans had developed a jet plane but did not exploit its full potential.